Wolves

LEVEL **3** READER

READING LEVEL
3
GRADES 2 TO 4

Written by Dalton Prescott
Illustrated by Colin Howard

113 Seaboard Lane, Franklin, Tennessee 37067. 1-866-418-2572.
No part of this book may be reproduced or copied in any form without written permission
from the copyright owner. CE16033/1212

The Wolf — A Survivor

The long, lonesome howl of a wolf brings to mind the American West. Yet very few of these amazing animals remain in the world, let alone in America. Once there were more than two million roaming the earth, but now there are about 200,000. Wolves were hunted to near extinction, but new laws protect this wild hunter.

Jackal

Dingo

Coyote

German Shepherd

The modern wolf comes from a long history of canines (doglike animals), and they are related to coyotes, jackals, dingoes, and domestic dogs. The first true wolves can be traced back more than a million years!

Wolves Around the World

Arctic Wolf

Eastern Timber Wolf

Northwestern Wolf

Great Plains Wolf

Red Wolf

Mexican Wolf

Wolf Tracks

The dire wolves (*Canis dirus*) appeared about 100,000 years ago in North America. Today, the remains of dire wolves are the most common canid fossils in North America.

Wolves used to live around the world, but they have disappeared in many places. Most now live in North America and Eurasia, and there are some in Europe and Africa.

Wolves have adapted to survive in many different environments. Those that live in colder climates have a thick fur coat to keep them warm. Wolves that live in warm climates have short, thin fur to stay cool.

Eurasian Wolf

Indian Wolf

Wolf Tracks

Several types of gray wolves live in Europe and Asia. *Canis lupus lupus*, sometimes called the Eurasian Wolf, roams all the way from France to China.

Born Hunters

This intelligent animal was made to hunt. Its most powerful sense is its sense of smell. A wolf can smell a moose over a mile away! A wolf's eyes are made to see in daylight and at night. And wolves have 42 teeth and a strong jawbone to capture their prey.

Wolves are strong, hardy hunters that cover large distances to find food, water, and shelter. They travel at about 5 mph, but may run for hours at a time. When they are chasing prey, they can sprint from 25 to 40 mph!

Lone Wolf Café

open All Nite!

Starters

Main courses

Desserts

Wolves make good predators because they adapt their diet to the food that is available. Wolves hunt large hoofed animals, like elk and deer, but they will also eat berries, fruit, and even garbage. They eat every part of their prey, including the organs and bones, to get the nutrition they need.

The Hunt

Wolves work together when they hunt, letting the young wolves watch and learn. First, the wolves locate prey with their strong sense of smell. They stalk the prey, following very quietly. This is followed by the encounter, when the prey is faced with the wolves. If the prey appears healthy and strong and stands its ground, the wolves may back off. If the prey seems weak and tries to flee, the wolves will begin the chase. As the wolves close in, they will rush at the prey, latching on with their powerful jaws, and bring the animal down. All of this takes planning and teamwork.

Most hunts are not successful because the animal gets away. Adult wolves can survive for weeks until they find another meal. When they do have a successful hunt, they eat quickly and gorge on the entire animal.

The Wolf Pack

Most wolves live, travel, and hunt in a unit called a pack. A pack is made up of two parents, their offspring, and sometimes a few outside members.

Wolf Tracks

Wolf packs can have as few as 2 members or as many as 30. The average pack size is 6 to 8.

The parents are the leaders, or *alpha* wolves, of the pack. The other members of the pack must submit to the alpha wolves. These pack leaders tell the wolves where to go, when to hunt, and where to make a den.

Wolf packs are always changing. Old wolves die, new pups are born, and older pups leave the pack and become lone wolves. Life is hard for lone wolves. They have trouble finding food and must be on the lookout for predators. Eventually, a lone wolf will join another pack, or find a mate and start a new pack.

Wolf Pups

During early spring, many animals give birth. This means plenty of prey for wolves. Mother wolves are busy at this time selecting a den or sheltered place to have their own pups. The den must provide protection and have water nearby.

The mother wolf nurses her pups in the safety of the den for nine weeks. The father and the other pack members defend the den, protect the young new members, and hunt to feed the mother and her pups.

Birth to two weeks

Newborn pups are blind and deaf. Their eyes open at 10 to 14 days. They may growl a bit and make a high-pitched howl.

Three to four weeks

At three weeks, pups can play outside the den. By four weeks, they "play fight" and the mother can leave them alone for a few hours to hunt.

Two to three months

The pups can now eat meat provided by the adults. They are ready to begin learning about hunting and fending for themselves.

Four to seven months

At four to five months, the pups tag along for part of the hunt. At six months, they look almost like the adults. At seven months, the young wolves are active members of the pack.

Wolf Talk

What's the first thing your dog does when it meets another dog? It sniffs! The sense of smell is the dog's— and wolf's—most keen sense. Wolves give off scents that "talk," or communicate, to other wolves. This is just one way wolves talk.

Wolves use their tails, ears, and facial expressions to signal moods and emotions. Some signals say, "I'm afraid." Some say, "Back off!" And some say, "Let's play!" Signals also show which wolves are dominant, and which wolves are submissive.

Howling is another way wolves talk to each other. They howl to assemble their pack, to scare off intruders, or start a hunt. Wolves can howl alone, or as a group. A wolf howl can reach another wolf six miles away!

Confident

Face It

Wolves use facial expressions and the position of their ears to signal emotion. Erect ears with a relaxed, closed mouth probably mean the wolf feels confident. A tongue that is showing might signify friendliness. Lowered ears indicate submission. A direct stare, wrinkled nose, and bared teeth are signs of potential aggression.

Submissive

Friendly

Aggressive

Gray Wolves

There are three species of wolves left in the world—*Canis lupus* (the gray wolf), *Canis rufus* (the red wolf), and *Canis simensis* (the Ethiopian wolf). Of these, the gray wolf is the most widespread.

Gray wolves are not always gray. They can be black, all white, or multi-colored, with mixtures of gray, buff, and red.

Wolf Tracks

In Scandinavia, a wolf chased by dogs and hunters was reported to have traveled 125 miles in one day and one night.

Northwestern Wolf

The northwestern wolf is also called the Alaskan or Mackenzie Valley wolf. It roams western Canada and Alaska, where it is legally hunted. These wolves were also reintroduced into Idaho and Yellowstone National Park in the 1930s.

The northwestern wolf is usually gray or black, but it can also be white, tan, or blue-ish. These wolves travel in packs of up to 30 wolves!

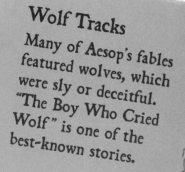

Wolf Tracks

Many of Aesop's fables featured wolves, which were sly or deceitful. "The Boy Who Cried Wolf" is one of the best-known stories.

Eastern Timber Wolf

The first gray wolf in the United States was the eastern timber wolf. It lived in the northeastern states until the early 1900s. Now it is almost extinct in the United States, but still lives in Canada. This wolf is smaller than other gray wolves, and zoologists think that it might be more closely related to the red wolf.

Wolf Tracks

More than 30 million years ago, in what's now the western United States, the mongoose-like Hesperocyon hunted. The size of a small fox, it was the earliest member of the dog family.

Great Plains Wolf

The Great Plains wolf lives in the western Great Lakes area in the United States and Canada. This wolf used to be very common, but now there are very few left in the western United States. The coat of the Great Plains wolf can be gray, black, or buff, with some red mixed in. These hardy wolves can roam far in search of prey like white tailed deer, moose, beaver, and birds.

Mexican Wolf

The Mexican wolf is the most distinct, rarest, and smallest North American gray wolf. It is only 4½ to 5½ feet long. Its coat is a mix of gray, buff, red, and black. Known as *lobo*, the Spanish word for wolf, the Mexican wolf is no longer found in the wild in Mexico.

Indian Wolf

The Indian wolf is mostly found in dry, desert regions of India and parts of Asia. It has a thin undercoat and a short outer coat to keep cool. Wolves that live in the desert can travel far to find food and water. They have special glands on their footpads that help them stay cool in the heat.

Wolf Tracks

The Indian wolf is not aggressive and may even appear to be semi-tame. Zoologists believe that domesticated dogs may have been bred from this small wolf.

Arctic Wolf

Arctic wolves are usually white and can travel very far to search for prey. They have adapted to their cold environment, which is sometimes 70 degrees below zero! Their large size, rounded ears, small muzzles, and short legs help them to stay warm. They also have long, thick fur and tufts of fur between their toes to keep them warm.

Wolves in cold climates have an outer layer of coarse hairs that work like a raincoat. This helps them to stay dry. It is hard to dig a den in such icy areas, so arctic wolves often live in caves and rocky areas.

Wolf Tracks

Winter white: Because white hair shafts have more air pockets than dark hairs, they may provide better insulation against the cold.

Wonder of the Wild

Since ancient times, humans have seen wolves as creatures of beauty, danger, and power. Wolves have played an important part in the folklore, legends, and art of many cultures. Our closest animal companion, the dog, behaves much like its wild brother. Is it any wonder that we watch in wonder at wolves?

The howl of the wolf may stir fear, but it also assures us that this cunning and amazing hunter still roams free.